JUST KEEP

Baking!

by
Taylor Merriam

Taylor's Tips & Tricks

- Allow eggs to come to room temperature (approximately 30 minutes) for fluffier baked goods.

- Allow butter to come to room temperature when baking (a few minutes on the counter) for a more tender cake/cupcake.

- Add a dash (approximate 1 Tsp) of espresso powder to any chocolate dessert to enhance the flavor of the chocolate!

- Trying to garnish that pretty dessert with strawberries - an egg slicer can double as a strawberry slicer for the perfectly sliced strawberries.

- Recipe calls for buttermilk but you only have regular milk? Whisk 1 TBSP of vinegar (or lemon juice if you don't have vinegar) into 1 cup of regular milk, let it sit for 5 - 10 minutes until slightly thickened, and voila, you have buttermilk. (Plain yogurt or sour cream thinned with a little bit of milk or water can also do the trick in a pinch).

- When making a decadent crème brûlée - use extra fine sugar for the brûlée for a more even top coat (Try vanilla sugar!)

- You just used a lovely vanilla bean for your decadent crème brûlée - DON'T throw that bean away! Make vanilla sugar! Place the bean in a small container of white sugar and seal. You now have vanilla infused sugar to make a lovely vanilla whipped cream or use as the top layer of your crème brûlée! Go crazy - vanilla sugar is so good on many things!

☆ Chocolate Chip Cookies - for a crispy edged cookie, replace 1/4 cup of the butter with 1/4 cup of vegetable shortening (think Crisco)

✪ Honey! Who doesn't love honey!? Honey can dress up just about anything from a lovely fruit platter to a decadent cheese plate! Plant something in your yard to attract honey bees to keep that lovely honey coming! Suffer from allergies? Buy local honey and ingest 1 TBSP daily to help relieve allergy symptoms!

✷ Store dry yeast in the freezer to help retain its lifting ability.

✩ Cookies seem a little flat? Check your dates on baking powder and baking soda!

★ Take full control of the sodium levels in your baked goods by always using unsalted butter!

☆ If you like fluffy cookies - roll your dough into a log and freeze. When ready to bake, slice the cookies and bake as described. The edges will bake before the middle is completely thawed and will result in a more fluffy cookie!

✷ Invest in an oven safe thermometer that attaches to your oven rack to ensure your oven temperature is always accurate.

✩ When baking - you MUST resist the urge to open the oven door! Opening the door releases the heat and changes the baking temperature. Use the oven light and the window instead!

✪ ALWAYS cool your cakes and cupcakes fully! If you're running short on time, place them in the refrigerator for 20 - 30 minutes (or the freezer for 10 - 15 minutes) before frosting.

Now let's start Baking!

TABLE OF CONTENTS

COOKIES

CHOCOLATE CHIP COOKIES

Ingredients

2 ½ cups all-purpose flour

1 Tsp baking soda

¼ Tsp baking powder

1 Tsp salt

1 cup softened butter

1 cup brown sugar

½ cup white sugar

2 eggs

2 Tsp vanilla

2 cups semisweet chocolate chips

Directions

Step 1. Preheat oven to 350°F. Sift together the flour and baking soda, set aside.

Step 2. In a large bowl, cream together the butter, brown sugar, and white sugar. Stir in the eggs and vanilla. Blend in the flour mixture. Finally, stir in the chocolate chips.

Step 3. Drop cookies by rounded spoonfuls onto ungreased cookie sheets.

Step 4. Bake for 10 to 12 minutes. Edges should be golden brown.

Step 5. ENJOY!

SUGAR COOKIES

Ingredients

2 ¾ cups all purpose flour

1 Tsp baking soda

½ Tsp baking powder

1 cup softened butter

1 ½ cups white sugar

1 egg

1 Tsp vanilla extract

Directions

Step 1.   Preheat oven to 375˚F.

Step 2.   In a small bowl, stir together flour, baking soda, and baking powder. Set aside.

Step 3.   In a large bowl, cream together the butter and sugar until smooth. Beat in egg and vanilla. Gradually blend in the dry ingredients. Roll rounded Tsps of dough into balls, and place onto ungreased cookie sheets.

Step 4.   Bake 8 to 10 minutes in the preheated oven, or until golden. Let stand on cookie sheet two minutes before removing to cool on wire racks.

Step 5.   ENJOY!

MACAROONS (GF)

Ingredients

3 egg whites

¼ cup white sugar

1 2/3 cups confectioners' sugar

1 cup finely ground almonds

Food coloring

Directions

Step 1.   Line a baking sheet with a silicone baking mat.

Step 2.   Beat egg whites in the bowl of a stand mixer fitted with a whisk attachment until whites are foamy; beat in white sugar and continue beating until egg whites are glossy, fluffy, and hold soft peaks. Sift confectioners' sugar and ground almonds in a separate bowl and quickly fold the almond mixture into the egg whites, about 30 strokes.

Step 3.   Spoon a small amount of batter into a plastic bag with a small corner cut off and pipe a test disk of batter, about 1 1/2 inches in diameter, onto prepared baking sheet. If the disk of batter holds a peak instead of flattening immediately, gently fold the batter a few more times and retest.

Step 4.   When batter is mixed enough to flatten immediately into an even disk, spoon into a pastry bag fitted with a plain round tip. Pipe the batter onto the baking sheet in rounds, leaving space between the disks. Let the piped cookies stand out at room temperature until they form a hard skin on top, about 1 hour.

Step 5.   Preheat oven to 285°F

Step 6.   Bake for about 10 minutes, until set but not browned; cool completely before filling.

Step 7.   Pipe your choice of filling

Step 8.   ENJOY!

LEMON COOKIES

Cookie Ingredients

1 cup softened butter

1½ cups sugar

1 egg

1 Tsp lemon juice

1 TBSP lemon zest

1 Tsp vanilla

½ Tsp salt

½ Tsp baking powder

2 cups flour

Lemon Glaze Ingredients

1½ cup powdered sugar

1 TBSP lemon juice

1 TBSP lemon zest

1 TBSP milk

¼ Tsp vanilla

Directions

Step 1.   Preheat oven to 350°F.

Step 2.   In a large bowl, cream butter and sugar together.

Step 3.   Add egg and beat in well.

Step 4.   Add lemon juice, lemon zest and vanilla and mix until well blended.

Step 5.   Add salt, baking powder and flour and mix until well incorporated.

Step 6.   Roll cookies into 1 inch balls and place on greased cookie sheet. Space cookie dough balls about 2 inches apart from each other.

Step 7.   Bake at 350°F for 8-10 minutes or until lightly golden on the edges of cookies.

Step 8.   Combine glaze ingredients in a medium bowl and whisk until smooth glaze is formed. Drizzle as much as desired over warmed cookies

Step 9.   ENJOY!

PEANUT BUTTER COOKIES

Ingredients

1 cup unsalted butter

1 cup crunchy peanut butter

1 cup white sugar

1 cup packed brown sugar

2 eggs

2 ½ cups all-purpose flour

1 Tsp baking powder

½ Tsp salt

1 ½ Tsp baking soda

Directions

Step 1.   Preheat over 375˚F

Step 2.   Cream butter, peanut butter, and sugars together in a bowl; beat in eggs.

Step 3.   In a separate bowl, sift flour, baking powder, baking soda, and salt; stir into butter mixture. Put dough in refrigerator for 1 hour.

Step 4.   Roll dough into 1 inch balls and put on baking sheets. Flatten each ball with a fork, making a crisscross pattern.

Step 5.   Bake for about 10 minutes or until cookies begin to brown. Let cool on wire rack

Step 6.   ENJOY!

DOG TREATS

Ingredients

1 cup rolled oats

1/3 cup butter

1 cup boiling water

¾ cup cornmeal

2 Tsp white sugar

2 Tsp beef bouillon granules

½ cup milk

1 egg beaten

3 cups whole wheat flour

Directions

Step 1.   Preheat oven to 325˚F

Step 2.   In a large bowl, combine rolled oats, margarine, and boiling water. Let stand 10 minutes. Grease cookie sheets.

Step 3.   Thoroughly stir in cornmeal, sugar, bouillon, milk, and egg. Mix in flour, 1 cup at a time, until a stiff dough has formed.

Step 4.   Knead dough on a lightly floured surface, mixing in additional flour as necessary until dough is smooth and no longer sticky. Roll or pat out dough to 1/2" thickness. Cut with cookie cutter (I prefer bone shaped), and place 1 inch apart onto the prepared cookie sheets.

Step 5.   Bake 35 to 45 minutes, or until golden brown. Cool before serving.

Step 6.   Let dog ENJOY!

I will love you forever Heaven ♥♥♥

4 PAWS FOR ABILITY · SINCE 1998

DESSERTS

STRAWBERRY CREAM CHEESE PUFF PASTRY

★ Taylor's Tip:
You can also use a heart cookie cutter instead of making rectangles!

Ingredients

1 package (1 ½ lbs.) fresh strawberries

2 sheets (8 ounce package) thawed puff pastry

5 ounces softened cream cheese

5 TBSP white sugar

1 1/2 Tsp vanilla extract

1 large egg, beaten for brushing

Confectioners sugar

Directions

Step 1.   Preheat oven to 400°

Step 2.   Line baking sheet with parchment paper of silicone mat.

Step 3.   In a small bowl, beat the cream cheese until smooth. Add a handful of diced strawberries, sugar, vanilla and mix till well combined.

Step 4.   Take thawed puff pastry and cut into 6 rectangles.

Step 5.   Use a fork and score the sides of the pastry.

Step 6.   Beat a small egg with whisk, and then brush the edges of pastry with a pastry brush.

Step 7.   Spread strawberry cream cheese mixture onto the center of each rectangle and top with additional fresh strawberries.

Step 8.   Bake for 16 minutes, or until golden brown.

Step 9.   Once cooled, dust with desired amount of confectioners' sugar

Step 10.   ENJOY!

MINI CHEESECAKE BITES

Ingredients

1 cup graham cracker crumbs

3/4 cup plus 1 TBSP sugar, divided

3 TBSP butter or margarine, melted

3 package. (8 oz. each) cream cheese, softened

1 TBSP brown sugar

1 Tsp vanilla

3 eggs

48 mini paper muffin liners

4 mini muffin pans

2 cookie sheets

Directions

Step 1.   Heat oven to 350°

Step 2.   In a medium mixing bowl, combine graham crumbs, 1 TBSP white sugar, 1 TBSP brown sugar, and 3 TBSP softened butter; and set aside.

Step 3.   In separate mixing bowl, beat 2 packages. softened cream cheese, 1 Tsp vanilla extract and ¾ cup sugar with mixer until blended. Add eggs, 1 at a time, mixing on low speed after each just until blended.

Step 4.   Press 1 Tsp graham cracker mixture onto bottoms of 48 paper-lined mini muffin cups.

Step 5.   Spoon cheesecake filling into each muffin liner.

Step 6.   Place two mini pans onto 1 cookie sheet, do this with the other two mini pans, and place both cookie sheets into the oven.

Step 7.   Bake 12-15 min. or until centers are almost set. Cool completely. Refrigerate 3 hours.

Step 8.   Top with your favorite topping or eat them plain.

Step 9.   ENJOY!

Taylor's Tip:
Use Kinnikinnick graham crackers for a Gluten Free alternative!

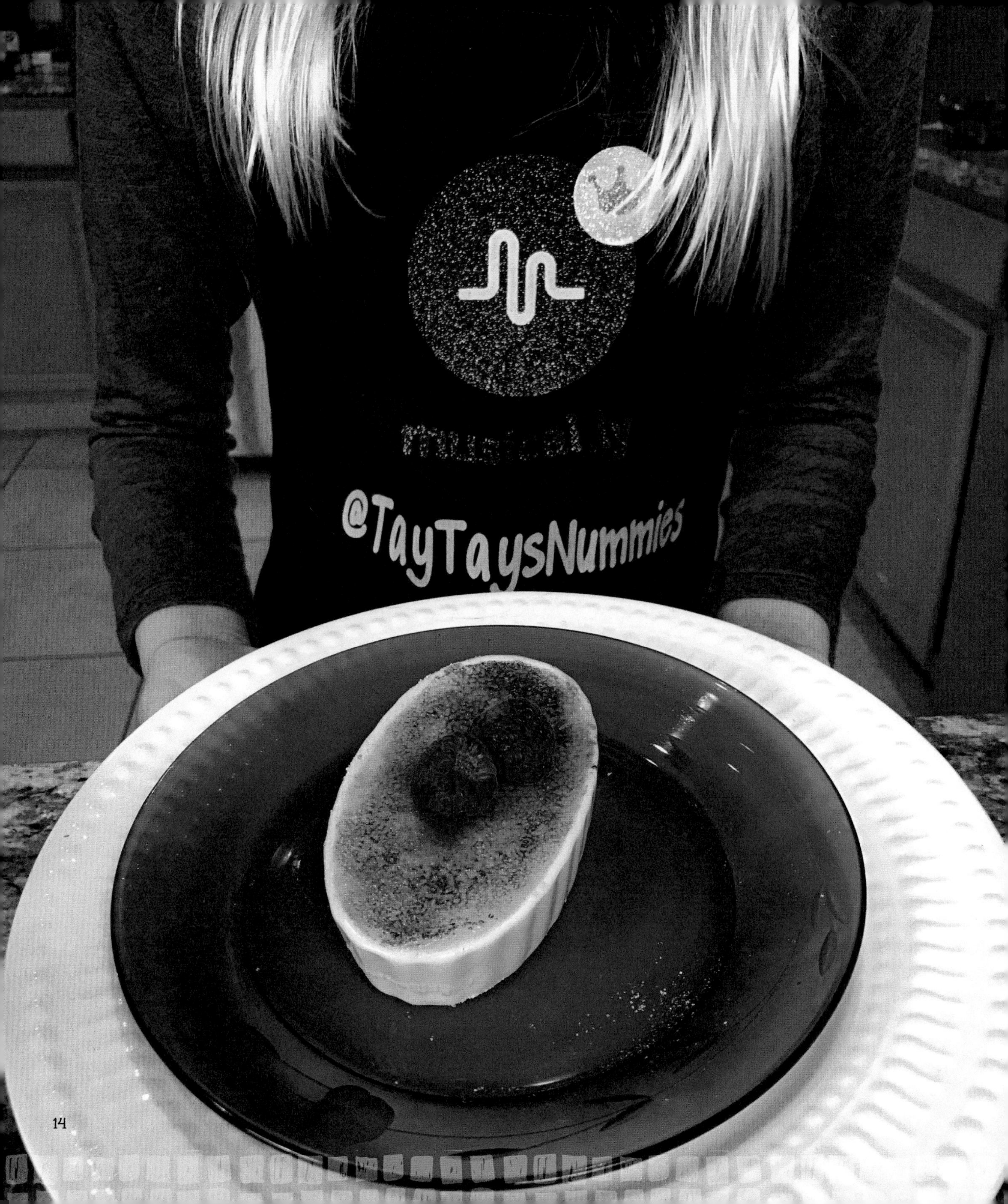
musical.ly
@TayTaysNummies

CRÈME BRÛLÉE

Ingredients

6 egg yolks

6 TBSP white sugar divided

½ Tsp vanilla extract

2 ½ cups heavy cream

2 TBSP brown sugar

Thank you
Nanny
for teaching
me how to
make Creme Brulee

Directions

Step 1. Preheat oven to 300°F

Step 2. Beat egg yolks, 4 TBSP white sugar and vanilla extract in a mixing bowl until thick and creamy.

Step 3. Pour cream into a saucepan and stir over low heat until it almost comes to boil. Remove the cream from heat immediately. Stir cream into the egg yolk mixture; beat until combined.

Step 4. Pour cream mixture into 6 to 8 ounce ramekins until almost full.

Step 5. Place the ramekins in a baking pan and carefully pour boiling water into the pan to come halfway up the sides of the ramekins.

Step 6. Bake for 35 minutes or until the custards are set when gently shaken. Remove the custards from the water bath, cool to room temperature, and refrigerate until firm.

Step 7. To serve, Preheat oven to broil. Or use a baking torch (but be very careful).

Step 8. In a small bowl combine remaining 2 TBSP white sugar and brown sugar. Sift this mixture evenly over custard. Place dish under broiler until sugar melts, about 2 minutes. Watch carefully so as not to burn.

Step 9. ENJOY!

MINI APPLE PIES

Ingredients

2 refrigerated pre-made pie crust, softened as directed on box

2 green apples, cored, finely chopped (about 1/4-inch pieces)

2 TBSP sugar

1 TBSP all-purpose flour

1/2 Tsp ground cinnamon

1 Tsp vanilla

1 egg

Directions

Step 1.   Heat oven to 425°

Step 2.   Remove both crusts from pouch; unroll on work surface. Using large round cookie cutter, cut out rounds. Gather up any scraps; re-roll with rolling pin and cut out more rounds to make a total of 20.

Step 3.   Press one crust round into each ungreased mini pie pan.

Step 4.   In medium bowl, stir together apples, sugar, flour, cinnamon and vanilla.

Step 5.   Pour apple mixture into pot and let simmer on medium heat until apples are soft.

Step 6.   Pour apple mixture evenly into each crust-lined mini pie pan.

Step 7.   Place remaining dough rounds over each mini pie, scoring edges with fork and using a knife to create little lines on top of each pie.

Step 8.   Bake for 16-20 minutes or until pastry is golden brown. Allow pies to cool for 10 minutes, then transfer to wire rack to cool before serving

Step 9.   ENJOY!

@TayTaysNummies

KEY LIME PIE

Ingredients

5 egg yolks, beaten

1 (14 ounce) can sweet and condensed milk

½ cup key lime juice

1 ½ cups finely ground graham cracker crumbs

1/3 cup white sugar

6 TBSP softened butter

1 Tsp grated lime zest (divided)

★ Taylor's Tip:
Use Kinnikinnick graham crackers for a Gluten Free alternative!

Directions

Step 1. Preheat oven to 375˚

Step 2. Combine the egg yolks, sweetened condensed milk. ½ Tsp grated lime zest and lime juice. Mix well and set aside.

Step 3. Mix graham cracker crumbs, sugar, melted butter or margarine, and cinnamon until well blended.

Step 4. Press graham cracker mixture into pie tin.

Step 5. Pour Key Lime mixture into unbaked graham cracker shell.

Step 6. Bake for 15 minutes. Allow to cool.

Step 7. Top with fresh whipped topping and garnish with lime slices and remaining lime zest.

Step 9. ENJOY!

CAKES & BARS

STRAWBERRY SHORTCAKE

Shortcake Ingredients

2 ¼ cups all-purpose flour

2 TBSP white sugar

4 TBSP baking powder

¼ Tsp salt

1/3 cup shortening

1 egg

2/3 cup milk

Topping Ingredients

2 packages (1 lb) fresh strawberries

½ cup white sugar

Whipped Cream Ingredients

1 ½ cups white sugar

¼ cup all-purpose flour

2 lemons juiced

Directions

Step 1. Slice the strawberries and toss them with ½ cup of white sugar. Set aside.

Step 2. Preheat oven to 425°F.

Step 3. Grease and flour one 8-inch round cake pan.

Step 4. In a medium bowl combine the flour, baking powder, 2 TBSP white sugar and the salt. With a pastry blender (or two knives) cut (add) in the shortening until the mixture resembles coarse crumbs. Make a well (hole) in the center and add the beaten egg and milk. Stir until just combined.

Step 5. Spread the batter into the prepared pan.

Step 6. Bake at 425°F for 15 to 20 minutes or until golden brown. Let cool in pan on wire rack. Set aside.

Step 7. In a large bowl, pour in and whip heavy cream until stiff peaks are just about to form. Beat in vanilla and sugar until peaks form. Make sure not to over-beat, cream will then become lumpy and butter-like.

Step 8. Slice cooled cake in squares, and top with whipped cream and strawberries.

Step 9. ENJOY!

CLASSIC LEMON BARS

Crust Ingredients

1 cup butter, softened

½ cup white sugar

2 cups all-purpose flour

Filling Ingredients

1 ½ cups white sugar

¼ cup all-purpose flour

2 lemons juiced

Directions

Step 1.   Heat oven to 350°

Step 2.   In a medium bowl, blend together softened butter, 2 cups flour and 1/2 cup sugar. Press into the bottom of an ungreased 9x13 inch pan.

Step 3.   Bake for 15 to 20 minutes, or until firm and golden, and set aside.

Step 4.   In another bowl, whisk together the remaining 1 1/2 cups sugar and 1/4 cup flour. Whisk in the eggs and lemon juice. Pour over the baked crust.

Step 5.   Bake for an additional 19 minutes. The bars will firm up as they cool. After both pans have cooled, cut into 2 inch squares

Step 6.   ENJOY!

BUTTERCREAM FROSTING

Ingredients

2 cups shortening

8 cups confectioners' sugar

½ Tsp salt

2 Tsp vanilla extract

1 cup heavy whipping cream

Directions

Step 1. In a medium mixing bowl, cream shortening until fluffy. Add sugar, and continue creaming until well blended.

Step 2. Add salt, vanilla, and 6 ounces whipping cream. Blend on low speed until moistened. Add additional 2 ounces whipping cream if necessary. Beat at high speed until frosting is fluffy.

Step 3. ENJOY!

ROYAL ICING

Ingredients

1/2 cup water

1/4 cup meringue powder

7 cups confectioners' sugar

2 TBSP light corn syrup

2 TBSP shortening

1 Tsp vanilla extract

Directions

Step 1. Whip water and meringue powder on high speed in a large bowl using an electric mixer until fluffy and soft peaks form, 7 to 10 minutes.

Step 2. Gradually add confectioners' sugar, shortening, corn syrup, and vanilla extract while mixing on low speed. Increase speed back to high and beat until well-combined and smooth, about 3 minutes

Step 3. Frost cooled cakes and ENJOY!

BROWNIES

Ingredients

½ cup softened butter

1 cup white sugar

2 eggs

1 Tsp vanilla extract

1/3 cup unsweetened cocoa powder

½ cup all purpose flour

¼ Tsp baking powder

¼ Tsp salt

Nuts (if desired)

Directions

Step 1.   Preheat oven to 350°F

Step 2.   Grease and flour an 8-inch square pan.

Step 3.   In a large saucepan, melt 1/2 cup butter.

Step 4.   Remove from heat, and stir in sugar, eggs, and 1 Tsp vanilla.

Step 5.   Beat in 1/3 cup cocoa, 1/2 cup flour, salt, and baking powder.

Step 6.   Spread batter into prepared pan.

Step 7.   Bake for 25 to 30 minutes or until a toothpick inserted into the brownie pan comes out clean.

Step 8.   ENJOY!

CHOCOLATE CUPCAKES

Ingredients

1 1/3 cups all-purpose flour

¼ Tsp baking soda

2 Tsp baking powder

¾ cup unsweetened cocoa powder

1/8 Tsp salt

3 Tbsp softened butter

1 ½ cups white sugar

2 eggs

¾ Tsp vanilla extract

1 cup milk

Directions

Step 1.　Preheat oven to 350 degrees

Step 2.　Line a muffin tin with paper baking cups.

Step 3.　Sift together the flour, baking powder, baking soda, cocoa and salt. Set aside.

Step 4.　In a large bowl, cream together the butter and sugar until light and fluffy. Add the eggs one at a time, beating well with each addition, then stir in the vanilla. Add the flour mixture alternately with the milk; beat well. Fill the muffin cups 3/4 full.

Step 5.　Bake for 15 to 17 minutes or until a toothpick inserted into the cake comes out clean.

Step 6.　Cool and frost.

Step 7.　ENJOY!

CHOCOLATE FROSTING

Ingredients

2 ¾ cups confectioners' sugar

6 TBSP unsweetened cocoa powder

6 TBSP softened butter

5 TBSP evaporated milk

1 vanilla extract

Directions

Step 1.　In a medium bowl, sift together the confectioners' sugar and cocoa, and set aside.

Step 2.　In a large bowl, cream butter until smooth, then gradually beat in sugar mixture alternately with evaporated milk. Blend in vanilla. Beat until light and fluffy. If necessary, adjust consistency with more milk or sugar.

CAKES IN A CONE

Ingredients

1 package cake mix

24 flat bottomed ice cream cones

Directions

Step 1.   Preheat oven and prepare cake mix according to directions.

Step 2.   Fill each cone about ¾ full of batter, up to first ridge.

Step 3.   Carefully place cones on a cookie sheet.

Step 4.   Bake at 400°For 15 – 18 minutes.

Step 5.   Let cool for 20 minutes and then top with unicorn ice cream or regular frosting.

Step 6.   ENJOY!

VANILLA CUPCAKES

Ingredients

2/3 cup softened butter

¾ cup superfine sugar

1 ½ cups self-rising flour

3 eggs

1 Tsp vanilla extract

Directions

Step 1. Preheat oven to 350°F

Step 2. Line muffin tin with paper baking cups.

Step 3. In a large bowl, mix butter and sugar until light and fluffy, for 5 minutes. Stir in the eggs, one at a time, blending well after each one. Stir in the vanilla and flour just until mixed. Spoon the batter into the prepared cups, dividing evenly.

Step 4. Bake 18 to 20 minutes. or until a toothpick inserted into the cake comes out clean.

Step 5. Cool and frost.

Step 6. ENJOY!

VANILLA FROSTING

Ingredients

½ cup unsalted softened butter

1 ½ Tsp vanilla extract

4 cups confectioners' sugar sifted

2 TBSP milk

Directions

Step 1. Cream room temperature butter until smooth and fluffy. Gradually beat in confectioners' sugar until fully incorporated. Beat in vanilla extract.

Step 2. Pour in milk and beat for an additional 3-4 minutes. Add food coloring, if using, and beat for thirty seconds until smooth or until desired color is reached.

RAINBOW UNICORN CUPCAKES

Ingredients

2 ½ cups all-purpose flour

2 Tsp baking powder

½ Tsp baking soda

½ Tsp salt

½ cup milk

½ cup olive oil

1 Tsp vanilla extract

½ cup butter

1 cup white sugar

3 eggs

Red, blue, green and yellow food coloring

⭐ *Taylor's Tip:*

To make cupcakes look like unicorns, take yellow fondant and roll out a long thin, snake-like piece and wrap it around a toothpick. For the ears, cut a small piece of white fondant into a triangle, use a butter knife to make a little line in the middle of the triangle to make it look like the center of the ear, and place it on top of the cupcake!

Directions

Step 1.   Preheat oven to 350°F

Step 2.   Line two 12 cup muffin pans with paper baking cups.

Step 3.   Stir together the flour, baking powder, baking soda, and salt in a large bowl. Whisk together milk, oil, and vanilla extract in a separate bowl until evenly blended; set aside.

Step 4.   Beat the butter and sugar until light and fluffy. The mixture should be noticeably lighter in color. Add eggs one at a time, allowing each egg to blend into the butter mixture before adding the next. Pour in the flour mixture alternately with the milk mixture, mixing until just incorporated.

Step 5.   Divide the cake batter into four separate bowls. Add a few drops of food coloring into one bowl of batter and stir; add more food coloring, to reach the desired shade. Repeat with the remaining colors and batter.

Step 6.   Using a different spoon for each color batter, spoon a small spoonful of each color into the cupcake liners, until 1/2 to 3/4 full. Do not mix the batter once it is in the cupcake liner.

Step 7.   Bake 15 to 20 minutes or until a toothpick inserted into the cake comes out clean.

Step 8.   Frost with fluffy vanilla frosting to make like a cloud.

Step 9.   ENJOY!

GLOW-IN-THE-DARK CUPCAKES

Ingredients

Cupcakes

White frosting

Tonic water

Lime jello

Black light

Directions

Step 1.   Frost cupcakes using white frosting with a star tip.

Step 2.   Put cupcakes in freezer while making the jello.

Step 3.   Mix lime jello with 1 cup boiling water and stir about 2 minutes until dissolved.

Step 4.   Add 1 cup tonic water to the jello.

Step 5.   Fill large bowl with ice water and place the bowl of jello in. Continue to stir letting the jello to cool down, but not set. When the jello is cool to the touch, remove it from the ice water.

Step 6.   Remove a couple of cupcakes at a time from the freezer and dip into the jello. Place them back into the freezer for 5 minutes. Repeat this dipping – freezing process 6 times. Be sure to stir the jello each time and watch it so it doesn't start setting up.

Step 7.   Get your black light out, turn off the lights and check out your cool cupcakes.

Step 8.   ENJOY!

ICE CREAM CUPCAKES

Ingredients

2/3 cup softened butter

¾ cup superfine sugar

1 ½ cups self-rising flour

3 eggs

1 Tsp vanilla extract

1 container vanilla ice cream

Sprinkles

Directions

Step 1.   Preheat oven to 350˚F

Step 2.   Line muffin tin with 24 paper baking cups.

Step 3.   In a large bowl, mix butter and sugar with an electric mixer until light and fluffy, for 5 minutes. Stir in the eggs, one at a time, blending well after each one. Stir in the vanilla and flour just until mixed.

Step 4.   Drop 2 TBSP of batter into the prepared cups.

Step 5.   Bake for 8-10 minutes or until toothpick inserted into the cake comes clean.

Step 6.   When the cupcakes have cooled completely, Spoon about 1/2 cup of the softened ice cream into each cup and gently pack it into the cup. Cover and place in freezer until frozen, about 4 hours.

Step 7.   Frost the cupcakes with the frosting or whipped cream.

Step 8.   ENJOY!

WHOOPIE PIE ICE CREAM SANDWICHES

Ingredients

2 cups all-purpose flour

½ cup unsweetened cocoa powder

½ cup hot water

1 Tsp vanilla extract

1 Tsp baking soda

1 cup white sugar

1 cup butter

Ice cream

Sprinkles

Directions

Step 1.   Step 1. Preheat oven to 375°F

Step 2.   Cream together 1 cup of the butter or margarine and the egg. Add 1 cup white sugar, vanilla and hot water. Stir in the flour, cocoa, and baking soda and mix well.

Step 3.   Drop 1 spoonful of batter onto a cookie sheet, or a whoopie pie pan.

Step 4.   Bake at 375°F for 10-12 minutes. Let cool 10-20 minutes. Set aside.

Step 5.   Take out your favorite ice cream and spread between the flat side of two whoopee pie cookies and sandwich together.

Step 6.   Quickly, roll the sides of the cookie into a bowl of sprinkles (ice cream melts fast).

Step 7.   Freeze 1 hour or until sandwiches are nice and firm.

Step 8.   ENJOY!

CHOCOLATE PEANUT BUTTER CUPS

Ingredients

1 cup melted butter

2 cups graham cracker crumbs

2 cups confectioners' sugar

1 cup peanut butter

1 ½ cups semisweet chocolate chips

4 TBSP peanut butter

Directions

Step 1.   In a medium bowl, mix together the butter or margarine, graham cracker crumbs, confectioners' sugar, and 1 cup peanut butter until well blended. Press evenly into the bottom of an ungreased muffin tin.

Step 2.   In a metal bowl over simmering water, or in the microwave, melt the chocolate chips with 4 TBSP peanut butter, stirring occasionally until smooth. Pour over the prepared crust. Refrigerate for at least one hour before serving.

Step 3.   ENJOY!

UNICORN NO-CHURN ICE CREAM

Ingredients

4 cups heavy whipping cream

2 cans (14 ounces) sweetened condensed milk

2 TBSP vanilla extract

Food coloring (pink, orange, yellow, green, blue & purple)

Directions

Step 1.   Empty two 14 ounce cans of sweetened condensed milk into a large bowl.

Step 2.   In a separate bowl, whip heavy cream to stiff peaks.

Step 3.   Slowly fold the whipped cream into the sweetened condensed milk, until all the whipped cream added.

Step 4.   Add 2 Tbs. vanilla extract and mix slowly.

Step 5.   Divide mixture into 6 small bowls and add desired food coloring to each bowl (in this recipe I used neon colors).

Step 6.   Layer each color into a 15x10 glass baking dish. Cover and freeze for 5 hours.

Step 3.   ENJOY!

Taylor's Tip:
This goes great with the Cake-in-a-Cone on page 29!

41

UNICORN POPCORN

Ingredients

6 cups popped popcorn

1 can pink food spray

1 12-ounce bag bright pink candy melts

1 12-ounce bag bright white candy melts

1 12-ounce bag blue candy melts

2 Tsp coconut oil

Pastel sprinkles

Pastel candy-coated chocolates

Directions

Step 1.   Place 1 TBSP of coconut oil and 6 cups popcorn in medium sized pot and cover, shaking pot till popping slows down. Set aside.

Step 2.   Lay the popcorn on cookie sheets and spray lightly with the pink food spray. Flip over and coat the other side. Set aside to dry as you prep the candy melts.

Step 3.   Place different colored candy melts into separate microwave-safe bowls. Heat for 25 seconds, stir, and reheat as needed. Stir in 1/2 Tsp or more of coconut oil to make the candy melts more loose and easily drizzled.

Step 4.   Drizzle candy melts over popcorn and top with sprinkles. Warm up candy melts, flip popcorn over and repeat, adding pastel candy-coated chocolates.

Step 5.   ENJOY!

GUMMIES

Ingredients

1 package (6 ounces) Candy flavored sugar free gelatin mix

6 envelopes unflavored gelatin

1.2 cup water

candy molds

Directions

Step 1.   In a saucepan, stir together the sugar free gelatin, unflavored gelatin and water until it resembles dough. Warm over medium heat until melted.

Step 2.   Pour gelatin mixture into molds, or if you don't have molds you can use a baking tray.

Step 3.   Refrigerate or freeze until firm, for 10 minutes.

Step 4.   Unmold or cut with cookie cutters and serve.

Step 5.   ENJOY!

UNICORN VS. SHARK MILKSHAKES

Ingredients

1 quart vanilla ice cream

1 cups milk

1 12-ounce bag bright pink candy melts

1 12-ounce bag of bright white candy melts

Pink food coloring

Blue food coloring

Blue & pink rock candy

Sour candy strips (rainbow and blue & red)

Colorful lollipops

Shark gummies

Pink and blue cotton candy

Sprinkles

Whipped cream

2 tall clear glasses

Long wooden skewers

Directions

Step 1. Separate ingredients and candy for each milkshake.

Step 2. Place different colored candy melts into separate microwave-safe bowls. Heat for 25 seconds, stir, and reheat as needed.

Step 3. Take each glass and quickly roll the top of the glasses into the candy mixture, and immediately roll into bowl of sprinkles.

Step 4. Pour ½ cup milk and vanilla ice cream into blender, adding desired food coloring each time.

Step 5. Decorate each milkshake to match your theme. For the long candy strips, fold them over in small sections and place wooden skewer through, then pull it down keeping it all in one piece.

Step 6. Top with whipped cream.

Step 7. ENJOY!

CLASSIC FRESH LEMONADE

Ingredients

1 ¾ cups white sugar

8 cups water

1 ½ cups lemon juice

Directions

Step 1.   In a small saucepan, combine sugar and 1 cup water. Bring to boil and stir to dissolve sugar. Allow to cool to room temperature, then cover and refrigerate until chilled.

Step 2.   Remove seeds from lemon juice, but leave pulp. In pitcher, stir together chilled syrup, lemon juice and remaining 7 cups water.

Step 3.   ENJOY with your best friend!

Thank you Lainey for being the best fundraiser ever!

BREAKFAST

BUTTERMILK PANCAKES

Ingredients

3 cups all-purpose flour

3 TBSP white sugar

3 Tsp baking powder

1 ½ Tsp baking soda

¾ Tsp salt

3 cups buttermilk

½ cup milk

3 eggs

1/3 cup melted butter

Directions

Step 1.   In a large bowl, combine flour, sugar, baking powder, baking soda, and salt. In a separate bowl, beat together buttermilk, milk, eggs and melted butter. Keep the two mixtures separate until you are ready to cook.

Step 2.   Heat a lightly oiled griddle or frying pan over medium high heat.

Step 3.   Pour the wet mixture into the dry mixture, using a wooden spoon or fork to blend. Stir until it's just blended together. Do not over stir! Pour or scoop the batter onto the griddle, using approximately 1/2 cup for each pancake. Brown on both sides and serve.

Step 4.   ENJOY!

WAFFLES

Ingredients

2 eggs

2 cups all-purpose flour

1 ¾ cup whole milk

½ cup vegetable oil

1 TBSP white sugar

4 Tsp baking powder

¼ Tsp salt

½ Tsp vanilla extract

Directions

Step 1.   Preheat waffle iron.

Step 2.   Beat eggs in large bowl with hand beater until fluffy. Beat in flour, milk, vegetable oil, sugar, baking powder, salt and vanilla, just until smooth.

Step 3.   Spray preheated waffle iron with non-stick cooking spray. Pour mix onto hot waffle iron. Cook until golden brown.

Step 4.   ENJOY!

CREPES

Ingredients

2 eggs

1 cup milk

2/3 cup all-purpose flour

1 pinch of salt

1 ½ Tsp vegetable oil

2 TBSP Nutella

Fresh strawberries

Whipped cream

Directions

Step 1. In a blender combine eggs, milk, flour, salt and oil. Process until smooth. Cover and refrigerate 1 hour.

Step 2. Heat a skillet over medium-high heat and brush with oil. Pour 1/4 cup of crepe batter into pan, tilting to completely coat the surface of the pan. Cook 2 to 5 minutes, turning once, until golden. Repeat with remaining batter. Cover and set aside.

Step 3. Cut up fresh strawberries (or favorite fruit).

Step 4. Open crepes and place desired amount of strawberries and whipped cream inside and roll crepe.

Step 5. Warm Nutella in a small ramekin in microwave for 15 seconds and drizzle over each crepe.

Step 6. ENJOY!

BLUEBERRY MUFFINS

Muffin Ingredients

1 ½ cups all-purpose flour

¾ cup white sugar

½ Tsp salt

2 Tsp baking powder

1/3 cup vegetable oil

1 egg

1/3 cup milk

1 cup fresh blueberries

Topping Ingredients

½ cup white sugar

1/3 cup all-purpose flour

¼ cup cubed butter

Directions

Step 1.   Preheat oven to 400°F.

Step 2.   Line muffin tin with baking liners.

Step 3.   Combine 1 1/2 cups flour, 3/4 cup sugar, salt and baking powder. Place vegetable oil into a 1 cup measuring cup; add the egg and enough milk to fill the cup. Mix this with flour mixture. Fold in blueberries. Fill muffin cups right to the top.

Step 4.   To Make Crumb Topping: Mix together 1/2 cup sugar, 1/3 cup flour, 1/4 cup butter, and 1 1/2 Tsp cinnamon. Mix with fork, and sprinkle over muffins before baking.

Step 5.   Bake for 20 to 25 minutes.

Step 6.   ENJOY!

TWISTED CHURRO DONUTS

Muffin Ingredients

1 cup water

2 ½ TBSP white sugar

½ Tsp salt

2 TBSP vegetable oil

1 cup all-purpose flour

2 quarts oil for frying

½ cup white sugar

1 Tsp ground cinnamon

Directions

Step 1.　In a small saucepan over medium heat, combine water, 2 1/2 TBSP sugar, salt and 2 TBSP vegetable oil. Bring to a boil and remove from heat. Stir in flour until mixture forms a ball.

Step 2.　Pipe strips of dough onto parchment paper, twist the strips and bring ends together to make a circle.

Step 3.　Heat oil for frying in deep-fryer or deep skillet to 375°F and place dough in one at a time. Fry until golden; drain on paper towels.

Step 4.　Combine 1/2 cup sugar and cinnamon into a bowl. Flip drained churros in cinnamon and sugar mixture until evenly coated.

Step 5.　ENJOY!

SAVORY SAUSAGE CRESCENTS

Ingredients

1 pound sausage

½ white onion

1 (8 ounce) package cream cheese

2 (8 ounce) packages refrigerated crescent rolls

Directions

Step 1.   Preheat oven to 350°F

Step 2.   Chop ½ white onion and set aside.

Step 3.   In a medium skillet, add sausage and onion and cook till sausage is lightly browned and drain. Once drained place back in pan, cover and set aside.

Step 4.   In a medium mixing bowl add cream cheese and sausage mixture, stir until cheese is melted and mixture is creamy.

Step 5.   Separate crescent rolls and place on workstation. Form log of sausage mixture horizontally across top of each triangle. Fold over the long sides of pastry to cover sausage mixture and roll down. Place on ungreased cookie sheet, seam down.

Step 6.   Bake 15- 20 minutes or until crust is golden. Let cool on wire rack.

Step 7.   ENJOY!

Thank you Mrs. Kay for teaching me to make these

NEW YEAR'S CUPCAKES

Ingredients

24 frosted cupcakes

24 Oreo cookies

Black food safe marker/pen

Directions

Step 1.   Place frosted cupcakes on workstation.

Step 2.   Carefully remove one side of the Oreo cookies, exposing the frosting. If cookie crumbs are present on the frosting, use a sharp knife to carefully scrape a thin layer off of the frosting, removing the crumbs with it.

Step 3.   Using a food safe marker or pen, draw a clock face onto the frosting of the Oreo cookies. Place cookie clocks on top of frosted cupcakes.

Step 4.   For an added touch, when presenting cupcakes put a sparkler on one cupcake and watch everyone's face light up with excitement.

Step 5.   ENJOY!

VALENTINE'S DAY STAINED GLASS HEART SUGAR COOKIES

Ingredients

2/3 cup butter

1 cup white sugar

½ Tsp vanilla extract

2 eggs

3 cups all-purpose flour

2 Tsp baking powder

½ Tsp salt

1/3 cup milk

40 fruit flavored hard candies

Directions

Step 1. Preheat oven to 350°F

Step 2. Grease cookie sheets.

Step 3. In a large bowl, cream together the butter and sugar. Stir in vanilla and eggs.

Step 4. In another bowl, sift together flour, baking powder and salt; add to egg mixture alternately with milk.

Step 5. On a lightly floured surface, roll the dough 1/4 inch thick. Cut into 1/4 to 1/2-inch-wide strips and, on a well-buttered baking sheet, form into window frames.

Step 6. Keeping the colors separate, place candy in plastic bags and crush with a meat mallet. Place crushed candies inside window frames.

Step 7. Bake for six minutes, or until candy is just melted. Cool on baking sheet for 5 minutes, until candy is hard. Carefully lift cookies off baking sheet with spatula.

Step 8. ENJOY!

VALENTINE'S DAY CINNAMON ROLL HEARTS

Ingredients

1 can (13 ounces) refrigerated flaky cinnamon rolls with icing

½ cup fresh strawberries

Directions

Step 1. Heat oven to 350°F. Spray 9-inch round glass dish with cooking spray.

Step 2. Carefully unwind each roll into long strip of dough, leaving center coiled. Coil the unrolled end of each strip in toward center, making two equal coils. Pull middle of strip down to make a point, forming a heart shape; pinch point. Place in glass dish, points toward center.

Step 3. Bake 13 to 15 minutes or until golden brown. Cool 5 minutes before removing to cooling rack. Drizzle frosting over warm rolls.

Step 4. Cut a handful of fresh strawberries and place them in the center.

Step 5. ENJOY!

ST. PATRICK'S DAY RAINBOW WAFFLES

Ingredients

Waffle batter

Red food coloring

Orange food coloring

Yellow food coloring

Green food coloring

Blue food coloring

Purple food coloring

Directions

Step 1. Divide batter into 6 bowls and tint each bowl with a different color.

Step 2. Pour each bowl of waffle batter into a piping bag and cut off a small portion at the tip.

Step 3. Pre-heat waffle maker, spray with non-stick cooking spray (if needed). Once pre-heated, start in the center and pour a small amount of purple batter. Then in a circular pattern follow with the blue batter and repeat for the green, yellow, orange and red batter. Make sure to fill all of the deep pockets, but don't overfill or the batter will leak out.

Step 4. Close & cook waffle according to directions on your waffle maker.

Step 5. Once your waffle is finished cooking, cut it in half and add whipped cream to the bottom to make it look like clouds.

Step 6. ENJOY!

Taylor's Tip:
Ice cream makes for pretty (and yummy!) clouds!

ST. PATRICK'S DAY GREEN PANCAKES

Ingredients

3 cups all-purpose flour

3 TBSP white sugar

3 Tsp baking powder

1 ½ Tsp baking soda

¾ Tsp salt

3 cups buttermilk

½ cup milk

3 eggs

1/3 cup melted butter

Cereal marshmallows

Green food color

Whipped cream

Directions

Step 1. In a large bowl, combine flour, sugar, baking powder, baking soda, and salt. In a separate bowl, beat together buttermilk, milk, eggs and melted butter. Keep the two mixtures separate until you are ready to cook.

Step 2. Heat a lightly oiled griddle or frying pan over medium high heat.

Step 3. Pour the wet mixture into the dry mixture, using a wooden spoon or fork to blend. Add desired amount of green food coloring and stir until it's just blended together. Do not over stir! Pour or scoop the batter onto the griddle, using approximately 1/2 cup for each pancake. Brown on both sides and serve.

Step 4. Top with whipped cream and cereal marshmallows.

Step 5. ENJOY!

EASTER/SPRING BUNNY CANDY BARK

Ingredients

1 12-ounce bag bright pink candy melts

1 12-ounce bag bright white candy melts

Black and pink food writers

Confetti sprinkles

Directions

Step 1. Cut 10 white candy melts in half (these will be your bunny ears).

Step 2. Use your markers and make 10 bunny faces. Set aside.

Step 3. Line baking tray with wax paper.

Step 4. Fill medium sized mixing bowl with pink candy melts and place in microwave for 90 seconds at 70% power. Stir and continue to heat at 30 second intervals until candy is melted.

Step 5. Pour melted candy melt into baking tray and quickly place your bunny faces and ears into the chocolate. Sprinkle with the confetti sprinkles and place in refrigerator for 1 hour.

Step 6. Take baking tray out and break apart with hands or use a knife to have clean edges.

Step 7. ENJOY!

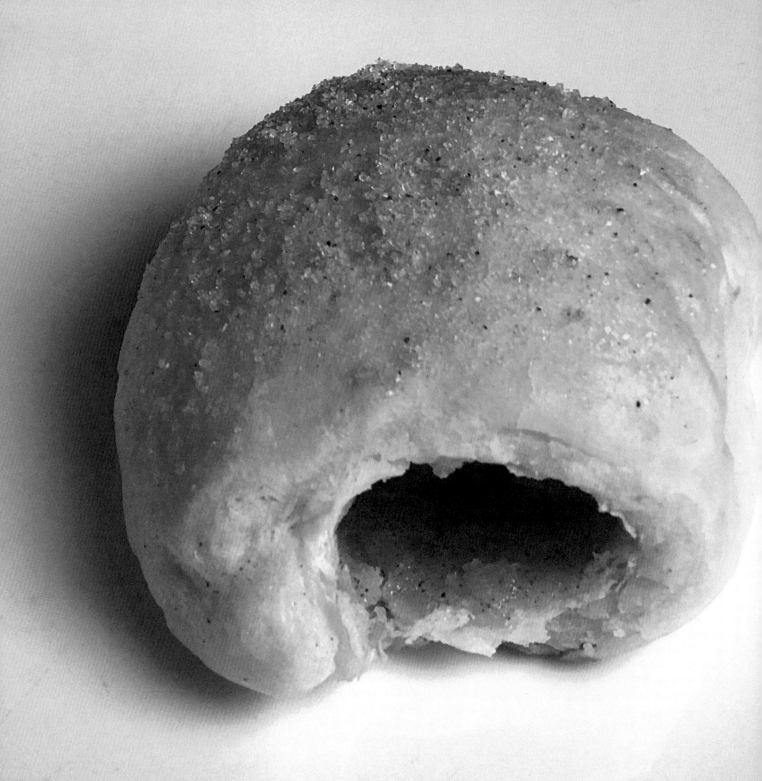

RESURRECTION ROLLS

Ingredients

1 package refrigerated crescent rolls

8 large marshmallows

¼ cup melted butter

2 TBSP ground cinnamon

2 TBSP white sugar

Directions

Step 1.　Preheat oven to 400°F

Step 2.　Lightly grease a baking sheet.

Step 3.　Separate crescent rolls into individual triangles.

Step 4.　In a small bowl, mix together cinnamon and sugar.

Step 5.　Dip a marshmallow into melted butter, then roll in sugar mixture. Place marshmallow into the center of a dough triangle. Carefully wrap the dough around the marshmallow. Pinch the seams together tightly to seal in marshmallow as it melts. Place on a baking sheet. Repeat.

Step 6.　15 minutes or until golden brown

Step 7.　ENJOY!

Taylor's Tip:
Sprinkle cinnamon sugar on top before baking!

EARTH DAY SUGAR COOKIES

Ingredients

2 ¾ cups all-purpose flour

1 TSP baking soda

½ Tsp baking powder

1 cup softened butter

1 ½ cups white sugar

1 egg

1 Tsp vanilla extract

Blue food coloring

Green food coloring

Directions

Step 1.   Preheat oven to 375°F

Step 2.   In a small bowl, stir together flour, baking soda, and baking powder. Set aside.

Step 3.   In a large bowl, cream together the butter and sugar until smooth. Beat in egg and vanilla. Gradually blend in the dry ingredients.

Step 4.   Divide dough evenly and place in separate bowls. Add 4 drops blue food coloring to one bowl, and 4 drops green food coloring to the other. Stir color till well combined.

Step 5.   Take a rounded Tsp of each color dough gently folding the colors together into balls, and place onto ungreased cookie sheets.

Step 6.   Bake 8 to 10 minutes, or until golden. Let stand on cookie sheet two minutes before removing to cool on wire racks.

Step 7.   ENJOY!

HALLOWEEN MUMMY COOKIES

Ingredients

Chocolate Chip Cookies

Candy eye balls

White frosting

Directions

Step 1.   Place all cookies on workstation.

Step 2.   Place candy eyes on all cookies.

Step 3.   Fill piping bag with white frosting.

Step 4.   Using a 44-flat decorating tip make horizontal lines from top to bottom.

Step 5.   ENJOY!

FALL MINI PUMPKIN PIES

Ingredients

2 prepared pie crusts

3 eggs (divided)

1 8 ounce softened package cream cheese

½ cup white sugar

1 cup canned pumpkin

1 Tsp vanilla Extract

1 Tsp pumpkin pie spice

Whipped cream

Directions

Step 1.   Preheat oven to 350°F

Step 2.   Roll each pie crust out onto a floured surface to a rough rectangle about 11 inches square. Cut each pie crust into 12 3-inch rounds. Fit the little pie crust circles into 24 mini pie dishes.

Step 3.   Separate one egg, and place the egg white into a small bowl. Beat the egg white until slightly frothy, and brush the edges of each mini pie crust with egg white. Place the remaining yolk into a bowl, and beat with remaining 2 eggs. Mix the softened cream cheese, sugar, pumpkin, vanilla extract, and pumpkin pie spice into the eggs to make a smooth filling. Spoon about 2 TBSP of the filling into each crust.

Step 4.   Bake the pies 15 minutes or until the crust edges are golden brown and the filling is set. Let cool.

Step 5.   Top with whipped cream.

Step 7.   ENJOY!

THANKSGIVING CINNAMON ROLL TURKEYS

Ingredients

1 can (13 ounces) refrigerated flaky cinnamon rolls with icing

10 slices bacon

1 package candy corn

1 package candy eyeballs

Directions

Step 1.   Preheat oven to 350°F

Step 2.   Take cinnamon rolls out of package and unwind the end of each cinnamon roll and tuck the end piece into the top of the roll.

Step 3.   Bake 13 to 15 minutes or until golden brown. Set aside.

Step 4.   While rolls are in oven fry bacon until firm. Set aside.

Step 5.   When rolls are warm (not hot) break bacon slices in half and slide 3 pieces of bacon in the back layer of each roll to make the feathers.

Step 6.   Pour frosting over the center of each roll and finish decorating eyes, candy corn nose.

Step 7.   ENJOY!

CHRISTMAS TREE BROWNIES

Ingredients

1 pan already made brownies

White frosting

Green food coloring

Mini candy canes

Yellow star sprinkles

Coloring sprinkles

Directions

Step 1. Take brownies out of pan and cut them horizontally in three rows. Then cut diagonally to make them look like triangles.

Step 2. Tint white frosting green and put into piping bag.

Step 3. Starting at the top of the tree, gently squeeze the icing out of the bag moving in a curvy zigzag as you go down the tree.

Step 4. Add your favorite sprinkles and red spicy candy and place a star at the top.

Step 5. Break off mini candy cane and insert it into the bottom of the brownie.

Step 6. ENJOY!

Taylor's Tip:
Use Inspiration Gluten Free Brownie Mix and prepare per package directions for a GF option!

CHRISTMAS SUGAR COOKIES

Ingredients

3 ¾ cups all-purpose flour

1 Tsp baking powder

½ Tsp salt

1 cup softened butter

1 ½ cups white sugar

2 eggs

2 Tsp vanilla extract

Directions

Step 1. Sift flour, baking powder, and salt together, set aside. In a large bowl, cream together the margarine and sugar until light and fluffy. Beat in the eggs one at a time, then stir in the vanilla. Gradually blend in the sifted ingredients until fully absorbed. Cover dough, and chill for 2 hours.

Step 2. Preheat oven to 400°F

Step 3. Grease cookie sheets. On a clean floured surface, roll out small portions of chilled dough to 1/4-inch thickness. Cut out shapes using cookie cutters.

Step 3. Bake 6 to 8 minutes, or until edges are barely brown. Remove from cookie sheets to cool on wire racks.

Step 4. Frost cookies.

Step 5. ENJOY!

THE MISSION OF THIS COOKBOOK

Since the beginning of Taylor's baking journey, she dreamed of having a cookbook to share with the world. While we were happy she had a goal like that we didn't anticipate it. Sadly, Taylor's Service Dog Heaven passed away November of 2016 and our hearts were broken. Heaven on many occasions saved Taylor's life by not only detecting before a seizure would strike but on a few occasions, she detected that Taylor had stopped breathing. While Taylor's seizures are not what they once were, she still has them so we are currently in the process of getting a new Service Dog from the same agency, 4 Paws for Ability. Because of this need in Taylor's life, we created this cookbook to not only facilitate her dream but also as a way to raise the money needed for this life saving dog. Please know a portion of all the proceeds to this book will be donated to 4 Paws for Ability - even after we meet our goal - so that other children and parents can receive the peace that comes from a highly trained service dog.

Matthew, Theresa, Taylor and Matt

Dear Parent, imagine your child having debilitating seizures on a sometimes-daily basis from the age of 3-10, now think about all the development that generally occurs during those years. For Taylor, most of that development didn't start to happen until she tried a medicine called Charlotte's Web and her seizures became controlled. This is when her life changed. This is when all of our lives changed and we all started living and experiencing life. This is when we began the journey of recovery which involved intense Speech therapy, Physical therapy, Occupational therapy, but most of all behavioral therapy. Each of these therapies played a role in her recovery but none matched what we gained from behavioral therapy and the HOPE it filled our hearts with. It is my heart's desire and prayer that Taylor's story will bring HOPE to families that have a child(ren) with special needs. These kids have so much potential, the key is to never give up helping them find their purpose in this world and in turn, the world will learn so much from them including, that they are not defined by a diagnosis.

`~ Mom (Theresa)

To say that the journey that has led us to the publication of this book was unexpected, would be a huge understatement. Several years back, the thought of our daughter, Taylor baking and interacting with thousands of people via social media would have seemed well beyond our scope of expectations. Having a front row seat on this amazing ride has been one of the most exciting times in our family's collective lives. More importantly, it has given us more than just joy but real-time hope that we no longer limit our own expectations and perceived limitations of Taylor's capabilities. The sense of pride, accomplishment and self-determination witnessed in Taylor has renewed our own often riddled with negative projections, forcing us to rethink the impossible: our daughter is learning life skills that will someday translate into our goals of her potentially being independent.

~ Dad (Matt)

FOREWARD

When I first met Taylor she was ten years old. She had been plagued with seizures from early in life. She had a diagnosis of autism and intractable Epilepsy. But, she had a wonderful enthusiastic family who was hopeful about helping Taylor grow and learn. At that time, Taylor only wanted to talk about her specific interests, and her favorite characters from her favorite shows. Her "pretend" play was limited to the scripts of shows and movies. This narrow range of interest also interfered with her ability to maintain friends. Her parents expressed their desire for her to develop an interest in something outside of her play-world with the hope that her friend-world could expand.

Teaching someone to be interested in something different than they are is not an easy task. I suggested to her mom that we teach her to bake by letting her choose a food that she loved, and have her bake it often - several times a week. In return she would earn uninterrupted free play with her favorite toys. The goal was that she would anticipate and memorize the steps (this also helping with her memory deficits), and receive praise and attention from mom for knowing what to do. And, each time she produced the yummy cupcakes (she chose cupcakes), she would experience the enthusiastic reaction of other people eating her treats, benefitting from positive social interactions, leading her to want more positive social interactions. It could be her entry into the world of friendship, and relationships with people.

What happened was beyond our wildest dreams! Several weeks after assigning the baking goal, Taylor and her mom sent me a picture of a recipe book she was creating for her family! Her idea! She wanted to produce a book for others. She asked to prepare more dishes. She enthusiastically considered options of things she could make, discussing it with her family! She discovered she loved to bake! She found out she wanted to make people happy! Baking turned out to be pivotal to Taylor's growth, connecting her to her family and eventually to her friends!

What you see here in the pages of this book are threads to happiness, opportunities for connections, and recipes which knit together community through yummy food. Taylor is now 12, enjoying the fruits of friendship, sharing her treats with you and developing connections through baking.

Bon apetit!

Tara Concelman is a Board Certified Behavior Analyst with a master's in education, who has a 29 year old son with Autism. Tara's life work is to teach caregivers and parents how to create for their children an environment in which their children can achieve success, using the principles of applied behavior analysis: the science of learning.

Tara is a Senior Behavior Analyst, and Parent Training Specialist for Positive Behavior Supports.

For more information about Positive Behavior Supports go to www.teampbs.com

Made in the USA
Columbia, SC
07 November 2018